Corporate Directorship Practices: The Planning Committee

by James K. Brown
Director, Management Planning and Systems Research

Ministry of Education, Ontario
Information Centre, 13th Floor,
Mowat Block, Queen's Park,
Toronto, Ont.   M7A 1L2

A Research Report from The Conference Board

658
.4012
B878

Contents

	Page
ABOUT THIS REPORT	v
FOREWORD	vii
1. THE CONTEXT OF A PLANNING COMMITTEE	1
The Case for a Planning Committee	1
Arguments Against a Planning Committee	2
Why Planning Committees Have Been Formed	2
A Useful Body	3
Why Planning Committees Have Been Rejected	3
2. WHAT PLANNING COMMITTEES DO	5
Capsule Descriptions	5
Other Contexts for Examining the Committee's Role	6
Specific Responsibilities	7
"Planning Plus" Committees	7
Relations with the Full Board	7
Changed Emphasis	8
3. MEMBERSHIP AND MEETINGS	10
Who Should Serve	10
Rotation of Members	12
4. DOES YOUR BOARD NEED A PLANNING COMMITTEE?	13
When Planning Committees Are Suitable	13
. . . And When They Are Not	13
Recap	14
APPENDIX: THE CORPORATE OBJECTIVES COMMITTEE AT TEXAS INSTRUMENTS INCORPORATED	15
EXHIBITS: STATEMENTS OF PLANNING COMMITTEE FUNCTIONS	16

Table

Details about Planning Committees	11

Author's Acknowledgments

It is my good fortune to have two colleagues, Jeremy Bacon and Rochelle O'Connor, who spend most of their working hours following the fields of corporate directorship practices and strategic planning, respectively. Both made informed and perceptive criticisms of earlier versions of the manuscript. Like service was performed by several study contributors, each of whom reviewed all or portions of the penultimate draft. Guaranteed anonymity by the ground rules under which Conference Board research is conducted, unfortunately they cannot be identified here. Finally, Lillian W. Kay, the Board's Manager of Editorial Services, did her customary adroit job of editing.

J.K.B.

About This Report

This report, latest in The Conference Board's series on corporate directorship practices, examines planning committees, a recent and as yet comparatively rare offspring of corporate boards. Sometimes instituted at the board's initiative, sometimes at management's, these committees commonly:

• Review mission statements, objectives, strategies and plans proposed by management.
• Monitor progress against plans.
• Evaluate the company's planning process.
• Discuss issues vital to the corporation.
• Advise the chief executive officer and other senior members of management.

The principal advantages of having a committee serve as the board's eyes and ears in planning matters, say those affiliated with such committees, are: (1) the smaller committee offers a more congenial forum than meetings of the full board for exploring these matters, and (2) the board has to transact too much other business for it adequately to fulfill its planning responsibilities.

Some executives and directors look askance at planning committees. The reasons: The board's role in planning for the enterprise requires the participation of all directors; a planning committee might prove to be disruptive; and service on it would add significantly to an already heavy workload for the members.

Outside directors form a majority of most planning committees—a pattern that conforms to that for longer established, more common board committees like audit, nominating and compensation. Whether or not a member of the committee, the chief executive typically attends at least some of its meetings. When the CEO does sit on a committee, it is rare for that individual to be chairman.

When Planning Committees Are Suitable

According to most study participants, planning committees are likely to be useful in certain business, organizational or management settings. For instance:

• When a new CEO takes office—especially if he or she comes from another organization, or must deal with a powerful predecessor who remains on the board.
• When management is not doing an adequate job of planning—whether through circumstances beyond its control or because of lack of self-discipline.
• When the company is confronted with revolutionary rather than evolutionary change.
• When a company has completed a major merger with a firm in a different industry.

On the other hand, a planning committee can well be beside the point if both management and the board are in accord about the future of the company and are content with the quality of the planning process.

Sample Selection, Research Design

Through reviewing annual reports and analyzing responses to earlier Conference Board directorship surveys, it was possible to identify about 40 board committees described in full or in part by the words "planning," "development," "strategy" or "objectives." Excluded from consideration were committees with such designations as "acquisitions," "mergers" and "diversification," which titles seem to suggest coverage of only part of the turf in the realm of planning.

The chief executive officers of most of the companies with committees that initially qualified for investigation were sent a brief questionnaire soliciting information on committee membership and functions. Such information was elicited about the other committees in interviews. As the research progressed, several additional planning committees were identified, and vital statistics about them were obtained. On the other hand, no effort was made to learn about the activities of committees with such titles as "finance" which, for some boards, reportedly perform most of the functions of a planning committee.

Those interviewed included outside directors who serve as planning committee members; chief executives, who spoke for their own boards and other boards on which they serve; and corporate planners. Also drawn on for this report were comments about planning committees made by speakers at Conference Board meetings and the as yet sparse literature on the subject.

Foreword

FOR MANY YEARS, The Conference Board has been studying and reporting on corporate directorship practices. Within the past two years we have published reports on audit and public policy committees; soon to appear is one on the nominating committee. The present report looks at the planning or development or similarly named committee. Although such committees are relatively rare, some observers believe they will become common as the trends to more vigorous and independent boards and to greater involvement of boards in planning and strategy continue. It seems appropriate, therefore, to ascertain why those committees that are now in place were formed, what they do, and who serves on them. The findings should be of interest to senior executives, directors, and corporate planners.

The Conference Board extends thanks to the company executives who completed questionnaires about their boards' planning committees and the members of such committees and corporate planners who shared their experiences and insights in interviews.

This study is a product of the Management Planning and Systems Research Department, a part of the Board's Division of Management Research, Harold Stieglitz, Vice President.

KENNETH A. RANDALL
President

Chapter 1
The Context of a Planning Committee

ONE CAN DISCERN mounting interest, in both management and academic circles, in the proper role of the board of directors in strategic planning for the firm it superintends. What contributions should it make to the determination of objectives, the fashioning of strategy, and so forth? Although this subject is not systematically examined here—this study focuses on the role and composition of board planning committees—the existence of such committees bespeaks recognition that the board has, or ought to have, some role in planning. And this larger question does provide a backdrop for an examination of planning committees.

In his seminal work, *Directors: Myth and Reality,* published in 1971, Professor Myles L. Mace found that, contrary to popular belief, a typical board does not get involved in the establishment of objectives, strategies and policies—an important bit of evidence for his myth versus reality theme.[1] Of course, a skeptic might argue that with respect to objectives and strategy there was precious little worthwhile activity anywhere in the corporation over the years when Mace did the research for his book.

In the decade since his book was published—and, some observers say, partly because of its publication—corporate boards have become more vigorous and more independent. And some have been concerned with those crucial elements of planning, objective setting and strategy development.

The Case for a Planning Committee

Defining strategy broadly as "the pattern of company purposes and goals—and the major policies for achieving those goals—that defines the business or businesses the company is to be involved with and the kind of company it is to be," Professor Kenneth R. Andrews (in a recent issue of the *Harvard Business Review*) has made a forceful plea for board involvement in strategy—and for a committee as a means for achieving this end.

"First, the board needs specific evidence that its management has a process for developing, considering, and choosing among strategic alternatives operating within the company.

"Second . . . especially if they have no personal experience in the industry, independent directors need to understand the characteristics of their company's business. Knowledge of strategy makes intelligent overview feasible.

"Third, knowing the company's strategy can give the board a reference point for separate decisions that come up before it and insights into what matters should be presented to it. . . .

"The fourth reason for directors to insist not only that a company have an explicit strategy but also that it present the strategy to them is that the evaluation of corporate strategy and of management's adherence to it allows continuous evaluation of management."

Andrews (and others) maintain that board planning committees are desirable, because, like other, more widely found board committees, they help the full board cope more effectively with an ever-growing work load. As Andrews puts it, "Organization by committee economizes the time of directors, puts the most qualified people in charge of given issues, educates directors, and provides a relatively private context for discussion of sensitive subjects."[2]

The case for a board planning committee can be put in the form of a syllogism:

Major premise: The board ought to be concerned with planning.

Minor premise: A planning committee is an effective mechanism for addressing this concern.

---

[1] Myles L. Mace, *Directors: Myth and Reality.* Boston: Harvard University Press, 1971.

[2] Reprinted by permission of the *Harvard Business Review.* Excerpt from "Directors' Responsibility for Corporate Strategy" by Kenneth R. Andrews (November-December 1980). Copyright © 1980 by the President and Fellows of Harvard College; all rights reserved.

Conclusion: It behooves a board to establish a planning committee.

The Appendix describes a board—that of Texas Instruments Incorporated—that is deeply involved in planning, and the role of that board's corporate objectives committee.

Arguments Against a Planning Committee

Given the paucity of board planning committees (see the description of sample composition and research design on page v), it is clear that the case for such a body is by no means widely accepted; far from it.

Responding to an earlier *Harvard Business Review* article ("Case of the Board and the Strategic Process," July-August, 1979), James L. Ferguson, chairman and chief executive of General Foods Corporation, argued against constituting a board planning committee in a letter to the editor of that publication:

> "It seems a legitimate role for board members to ensure themselves that the proper processes are in place for establishing broad strategic direction. It would not be my choice, however, to establish a committee for the purpose. Rather, I would have management discuss the process with the entire board and get its reactions, input, and, ultimately, understanding.
>
> "First of all, strategic planning processes are sufficiently important that all the directors should be involved in them and should understand them.
>
> "Second, a committee, particularly one that spends time meeting with members of the organization to gain insight, might be disruptive, and questions could arise about its true role.
>
> "Third, I am not sure that many board members could or would take the additional time required for such committee deliberations beyond what they already contribute. In our case, most of our directors already serve on two committees. We give them a good bit of material to review. My present concern really is more one of overloading than of seeking opportunity to add additional work."[3]

Another questioner of the benefits of the board planning committee is Charles S. Mechem, Jr., chairman of the board of the Taft Broadcasting Company and an outside director of nine other companies, the boards of two of which have planning committees on which he sits. In a talk, "An Outside Director's Perspective on Strategic Planning," at a Conference Board strategic planning conference held in March, 1981, Mr. Mechem made these points about the full board vis-à-vis strategy:

- The basic role of the board is to protect and enhance the shareholders' investment in the enterprise.

- The chief executive officer is the only proper architect of corporate strategy. Outside directors should assess that individual according to his or her ability to devise strategy and his or her commitment to carry it out. Regarding strategy, the function of outside directors is to review it and not make it. It is inappropriate for management and the board to devise strategy in tandem. If the board gets deeply involved in planning and strategy, it may overlook the welfare of the shareholders and it may fail properly to assess the chief executive.

The "workable areas of board involvement" in planning and strategy are:

(1) The board should insist that there be a corporate plan and its members should insist upon knowing what the plan is.

(2) The board should insist that there be a thorough and intelligent planning process.

(3) The board should take care to be promptly informed of dramatic changes that affect the plan.

(4) The board should know who are involved in the corporate planning effort and ascertain how competent these individuals are.

(5) The board should determine whether prior plans have worked out.

(6) The board should contribute to discussions of what businesses the company should be in, or at least satisfy itself that management is giving ample consideration to this question.

(7) The board must assure itself of the adequacy and availability of resources.

(8) The board should see to it that the fields of expertise of its members are fully utilized.

Turning to planning committees, Mr. Mechem observed that the problem with such a committee is that it is a disservice to directors who are not committee members. They are deprived of information they need to protect and enhance the shareholders' investment. The board should deal with corporate planning and strategy as a committee of the whole. (Two of the planning committees included in this inquiry are precisely that.)

Why Planning Committees Have Been Formed

Compared with Professor Andrews' statement of the case for planning committees, explanations by study participants of the origins of planning committees with which they are affiliated are, not surprisingly, more

---

[3] *Harvard Business Review,* November-December, 1979, pp. 230, 232. Reprinted by permission of the *Harvard Business Review.* Copyright © 1979 by the President and Fellows of Harvard College; all rights reserved.

pragmatic or expedient. Something appeared to be amiss or lacking; or the planning committee was looked upon as a worthwhile experiment; or, in at least one instance, the planning committee seems to be a product of evolution. Sometimes one or more outside directors, sometimes the chief executive, took the initiative in forming such committees. For instance:

- Because the management of a small but successful financial services firm is inevitably preoccupied with minute-by-minute decisions with enormous financial consequences, a committee of outside directors has been constituted to help company executives address long-term opportunities and problems.
- At an aerospace firm, it was the disappointing results of a management program to diversify into commercial businesses that led a group of outside directors to create a committee whose principal role has been to insist that management undertake a formal strategic planning program.
- Another board had felt that it had not been adequately drawn into the formulation and review of strategy during the tenure of previous chief executives. With the accession of a new one, it created a committee to correct this perceived deficiency.
- Recruited from another firm, the new chief executive officer of a company that had no formal planning initiated individual conversations with outside directors as to the proper future course of the enterprise. In one such conversation, either he or the outside director—no one is sure which—casually suggested that a planning committee might be useful. The other person thought it a good idea—and soon a committee was in place.
- Another chief executive, again an outsider, came to his position through leading a successful proxy fight against the previous management. Lacking hands-on experience in running a company—his background had been in investments and stock market trading—he asked two outside directors, themselves newly elected, to serve with him on a committee that would concern itself with the future direction of the company.
- Two mergers had caused one company to have a large and unwieldy board, at one time numbering 23 directors, with a profusion of committees. One unstated but clear function of some of them was to give committee assignments to directors who otherwise might not have had any. A planning committee without a clear mandate was included in the roster of this board's committees. As the board's size shrank through a planned program of attrition—it now numbers 10 directors—a consolidation of committees took place. The planning committee was combined with another, and this body now serves as an effective, institutionalized sounding board for management.

A Useful Body

Most of those interviewed expressed considerable enthusiasm for the planning committees with which they are affiliated. They claim that the committees have been beneficial to management and the board alike. Among the gains noted: Strategic planning has been launched, improved or sustained; longer range questions are receiving more attention than previously; management has more self-confidence; and the full board better understands the firm's businesses and feels more comfortable about the future of the enterprise. Why are these pluses attributed specifically to planning committees? For two interrelated reasons, principally. The smaller committee offers a more congenial forum than meetings of the full board for discussing planning issues (cf. Professor Andrews' comment on this point). And the board has to transact too much other business, business largely of a here-and-now nature, for it adequately to fulfill its planning responsibilities.

Of course, the effectiveness of any working group, whether a standing committee or an ad hoc body, depends in part on the adroitness of its chairman. This is particularly true if the group has been in existence for a short time and its mission or functions are not, or cannot be, precisely defined. Both conditions are more apt to apply to board planning committees than, say, to compensation or audit committees. More than one study participant has stressed the contribution of an imaginative and dedicated chairman to the development of a useful, constructive planning committee.

Why Planning Committees Have Been Rejected

This inquiry turned up two instances in which, at management's initiative, the establishment of a planning committee was contemplated but was eventually rejected.

One chief executive officer believed that such a committee would be a valuable addition to the structure of the firm's board. But the board vetoed his proposal, on the ground that its responsibility for planning was too important to be delegated to a committee. Enough said.

In the second instance, a corporate planner was asked to explore the question of greater involvement of the board in the firm's planning, including, perhaps, creation of a planning committee. Although the decision made was to defer action for the present, some of the planner's views may be relevant to others considering a similar change.

Engaged in highly technical businesses, the firm has been successful in terms of growth and profits. Its board is composed mainly of outside directors. As in many firms, the board presently receives summary presentations of plans for the firm as a whole and for its constituent units. Subsequently, as the units perform against plan, there are regular management reports comparing planned versus actual results, and indicating the actions taken to deal with significant variances. At both the plan presentations and the subsequent performance reports to the board, directors can and do raise questions relating to strategies, resources and risks. Clearly, the board is involved in the firm's planning.

The need for *greater* planning involvement must be viewed in relation to the primary responsibility of the board: to evaluate the company and its chief executive, and to provide adequately for management succession. While greater involvement may facilitate the discharge of these responsibilities, it also raises questions of a fundamental nature:

(1) What is the nature of the business and its risks?

(2) What should be the nature of the greater board involvement? What role should the board take in assessing risks? What added value is expected in terms of better decisions?

(3) What would then be required in terms of directors' skills, experience and time commitment to yield that added value?

Take the questions of risk and its attendant requirements on directors. Management, of course, is expected to make the strategic decisions for the firm—those major risk-bearing decisions that set the direction of the business and determine its long-term health. Since risk has many forms (such as marketing, manufacturing, financing, technical and political), it is useful to categorize businesses in terms of the risks normally taken.

Suppose firms facing primarily the risks of marketing, manufacturing and financing are designated as Category I firms; and those facing these risks as well as technical and/or political risks are designated as Category II firms. A regional manufacturer of camping equipment is an example of a Category I firm; a semiconductor firm with operations in many countries, a Category II firm. Category I firms face a world in which the pace of technology is moderate and in which the pressures of governments, while burdensome, are broadly applied (not, for example, aimed at nationalizing a firm's subsidiary). Category II firms, on the other hand, face a far more turbulent and trying world environment.

Looking at the pool of talent—bankers, lawyers, academics and CEO's from firms in other industries—one would expect that Category II firms will find fewer candidates with skills and experience suitable to their needs than will Category I firms. And Category II firms will place heavier demands on its directors than will Category I firms—that is, the directors will need on average to have both broad-ranging business perspectives and specialized knowledge in science or politics. Furthermore, if they are to add value in the firm's planning process, these directors must keep current on what is happening in these domains and what the firm's strategies are for dealing with the more complex problems or opportunities. This will significantly increase the amount of time and effort which directors must devote to board duties, possibly doubling the time spent on board matters.

These, then, are some of the problems to be addressed in increasing a board's involvement in corporate planning, whether or not this entails constituting a planning committee. With thought, effort and time, greater involvement can be achieved, and with it, the potential for better business decisions.

Chapter 2
What Planning Committees Do

IN *Directors: Myth and Reality,* Myles Mace described three functions commonly performed by boards of directors:[1]

(1) Providing advice and counsel to the chief executive—acting as a sounding board, as a window through which other points of view are brought to management's attention.

(2) Serving as some sort of discipline for management, which role grows out of management's recognition that periodically it must account to the board on the progress of the enterprise.

(3) Acting in crisis situations, notably when the CEO dies unexpectedly and a replacement must be designated, and when management performance becomes so unsatisfactory that a change in the chief executive must be made.

Mace's investigation led him to conclude that most boards do not perform three "generally accepted roles":

(1) Establishing the basic objectives, corporate strategies, and broad policies of the corporation.
(2) Asking discerning questions of management.
(3) Selecting the chief executive.

To varying degrees, the board planning committees surveyed for this report—and they were surveyed a decade or more after Mace did his research, an interval in which many corporate boards have become more assertive—appear to carry out two of the first three commonly performed functions. They give the chief executive advice and counsel, and they exert discipline on the chief executive and his management colleagues.

The committees also are involved in carrying out two of the "generally accepted roles" of the board. They ask

[1] Mace, 1971.

discerning questions of management. They participate, in varying degrees, in the establishment of the basic objectives, corporate strategies, and broad policies of the corporation. And while apparently none of them has as yet played a major part in the selection of a chief executive, those whose activities include surveillance of manpower planning and development may well do so in the future.

Capsule Descriptions

The several capsule descriptions of the role of their planning committees provided by individual committee members illustrate differing admixtures of these functions. These descriptions also reveal that the distinctions among the functions become blurred in practice.

Establishing objectives, and so on. At the company, a manufacturer mentioned on page 3, the three-person committee, consisting of the chief executive officer and two outside directors, is the only unit in the organization (there is no planning department) to dedicate itself exclusively to the firm's future direction and emphasis. In freewheeling, brainstorming sessions, the committee addresses such questions as: "What units ought to be disposed of?" "What units ought to be built on?" "What new businesses should the company consider entering?"

Establishing objectives, providing advice and counsel, asking questions. At an airline, the committee's formal function is to review business plans and financing plans and, with perhaps some modification, recommend their acceptance by the full board. But the committee chairman characterizes the substance of the committee's work as "continually considering options for the company, the best use of the shareholders' resources." To this end, the committee serves as a forum where management and committee members can fully and unhurriedly discuss issues of concern over a period of time. Committee members do not generate ideas, but rather react to those put forth by management and raise "tough questions."

Exerting discipline. At several companies, the main contribution of the committees has been to insist that the managements in question institute, or vigorously sustain, strategic planning programs. As noted in Chapter 1, it is the opinion of some study contributors that this is a role the full board cannot perform because it is fully occupied with other matters.

Providing advice and counsel, establishing objectives. At a manufacturer, an important, although unofficial, role of the committee has been to act as an advisory group to the chief executive officer, who himself is the committee chairman. Although officially the committee's task is to review management's plans and proposals, these documents lead to general discussions about the future of the company.

Establishing objectives, providing advice and counsel. In the early days of the four outside-director manufacturing company committee which he chairs, one respondent notes that the committee's role was to have management define the mission, basic objectives, and strategies of the company in such a way that the full board later could grasp them, endorse them, and measure performance against them. The committee has subsequently reviewed each stage of the strategic plan developed by management, including assumptions, and modified or eliminated what was not to its liking. Also, the committee has been concerned with other long-term subjects such as acquisition philosophy, organizational changes required by a series of acquisitions and divestitures, and the proper balance between national and international business for the company. One unanticipated role for the committee was to counsel management in the face of a hostile, and eventually unsuccessful, tender offer.

Establishing objectives, asking questions, providing advice and counsel. At a business services firm, the formal responsibility of the committee is to be "advisory and consultative to the board of directors and the chief executive officer." But the committee also participates in setting strategies through discerning questions and suggestions. It also monitors progress against plans.

Other Contexts for Examining the Committee's Role

The views of Robert K. Mueller, chairman of the board of Arthur D. Little, Inc., and a prolific writer about directorship practices, offer another context for examining the role of the planning committee. At a November, 1980, Conference Board meeting on "The Board of Directors: A Revamped Institution With A Tough Agenda," he suggested that there are four ways of looking at corporate boards:

(1) An intuitive model. This is the "traditional concept of the board which everyone understands, but which is inadequate."

(2) The classical model. In this model the functions of the board are (a) to give legitimacy to the corporation, (b) to provide an auditing or monitoring capability and (c) to direct (but not manage) the corporation. This model Mueller finds to be inadequate for very large and complex organizations.

(3) The process model. He distinguishes five processes:

(a) The statutory or fiduciary role defined by fixed, clearly stated laws and regulations, which the board performs well.

(b) The evaluative role, in which the board passes judgment on the performance of the chief executive and the company's performance vis-à-vis its competitors, industry norms, and strategic plans.

(c) The participative role—a controversial one—in which the board gets involved in functions management performs and thus delicately invades management's turf or "gently pierces the veil between management and the board." Examples of the participative role are the work of the auditing, nominating, compensation and planning committees of the board.

(d) The resource or consulting role. This is the reverse of the participative role. Here management asks the board for help.

(e) The catalytic or change-agent role—the "model of the future" according to Mueller. For instance, the board performs this role when it determines that the company should go in a different direction from what management has recommended—whether it takes action in a crisis or a noncrisis situation.

(4) The systems role. An important distinction, Mueller finds, is that management is a closed system of command and control, with fixed and rigid boundaries, whereas the board is, or ought to be, an open system, with loose and permeable boundaries. Mueller notes that a CEO, accustomed to a closed system in his organization, sometimes feels uncomfortable acting as an outside director in a more open boardroom system.

It seems clear that board planning committees, in carrying out the functions described earlier in this chapter, transcend the intuitive model. With respect to the classical model, planning committees do provide an auditing and monitoring capacity and do participate in the direction of the corporation. In the process model, all the committees contributing to this study clearly play an evaluative role; some play a participative role; and a few have, on occasion, played a change-agent role. Finally, in the systems model, at least those committees that have been in existence for some time and are functioning vigorously can be classified as open systems.

Professor Mace, a co-panelist of Mr. Mueller's at this conference, observed that there is no institutionalized, generally accepted set of principles about the role of outside directors, which is why there is such a wide variety of practices in the substantive work of corporate boards. Very few companies have attempted to establish such a set of principles for their own managements and boards. What is needed is to define the role of the board, to develop a clear understanding about the proper relationship between the chief executive officer and outside directors, so each party fully grasps the expectations of the other. In the aura of uncertainty about board-management relationships described by Professor Mace, the planning committee can perhaps be looked upon as a mechanism for clarifying these expectations.

Specific Responsibilities

An analysis of the written statements of planning committee responsibilities reproduced at the end of the report reveals that the most common committee functions, in order of frequency of mention, are:

(1) Reviewing mission statements, objectives, strategies, plans;
(2) Monitoring progress against plans;
(3) Evaluating the company's planning process;
(4) Discussing issues vital to the corporation;
(5) Advising the chief executive officer and, in some cases, other members of management.

This list corroborates a point often made by members of board planning committees as they talk about what their committees do. The predominant committee function is that of review. It is not one of formulation or proposal. It is management's job to devise objectives and strategies, to prepare plans. The committee (or in the absence of a committee, the full board) should confine itself to accepting, modifying or rejecting management's recommendations.

But something more comes through in conversations with planning committee members. Through their pointed questions—for example, Have you thought of this or that? Don't you think we should consider disposing of the XYZ division?—through questions such as these, their directors are not merely reactive in setting objectives, strategy development and the like.

At least two committees are formally charged with taking an activist stance, though the relevant language in the second committee's charter is a bit enigmatic:

"The committee shall be on the alert and make appropriate recommendations for potential new business opportunities" (see Exhibit 7).

"Resolved that the policy and planning committee shall . . . be prepared to become involved in specific major and critical business situations where the company might benefit from the experience and perspective of the members" (see Exhibit 13).

On the other hand, the same committee's chairman is proscribed from impinging on management's prerogatives:

"It is recognized that the chairman of the policy and planning committee must keep informed and be kept informed of developments of significance in the company and that he will have direct communication with appropriate staff, but that such communication will not interfere with or hinder the chief executive officer in fulfilling his responsibilities. . . ."

A similar but somewhat broader constraint applying to the full committee appears in another committee's charter:

"It is not the purpose of this committee to assume any of management's responsibility for the day-to-day functioning of the company" (see Exhibit 3).

"Planning Plus" Committees

Several planning committees are charged with other tasks that seem, to a greater or lesser degree, to be discrete from corporate or strategic planning. At a manufacturing company there is a corporate planning and nominating committee. An airline has a finance and planning committee. A business services firm and a bank both have a policy and planning committee.

A few of the committees surveyed combine strategic planning responsibilities with manpower planning or development (see Exhibits 3 and 12). The chairman of two of these committees, an individual long prominent in the field of business education, asserts that this marriage is essential and insists that it be made on any board on which he sits. The two most important jobs of a chief executive officer, he says, are to plan the future of the enterprise and to make sure that there is, and will continue to be, competent manpower in place to realize this future. For the board to be effective in fulfilling its responsibilities regarding these vital and interrelated functions, he maintains that it should have a single committee overseeing both.

One participant contends that, whatever its formal charge, a planning committee will inevitably get involved in the issue of management succession, particularly succession to the chief executive officer's job. For an analysis of manpower within the organization is integral to sound strategic planning. Another study contributor stresses the role his committee plays in management appraisal: It can, and does, "measure a man well" by the quality of the presentations he makes to it.

Relations with the Full Board

A planning committee is, after all, a creature of the full board. What, then, is the relationship between such a committee and the full board?

An earlier Conference Board report described the role of board committees:

"Board committees serve different functions, depending on the nature of the responsibility involved and the amount of authority delegated to the committee by the board. Perhaps the most basic function of most board committees, other than executive committees, is to be fact-finding bodies—to serve as the eyes and ears of the full board in particular areas of corporate affairs—and, in turn, to keep the board informed, either through reports or minutes of committee meetings, or both. Another function that may be delegated to a board committee is that of monitoring corporate operations or performance in a specified area; this is often a prime responsibility of the audit committee, for example, which is usually charged with seeing to it that the corporation's financial reporting and controls are all they should be.

"A committee may also be charged with the further responsibility of going beyond fact-finding or monitoring and arriving at conclusions in the form of recommendations to the full board that action be taken. Finally, a committee may be empowered to act for the full board on some matters—usually, but not always, subject to later confirmation by the full board. . . ."[2]

It appears that planning committees perform all but the last of these functions. They do "serve as the eyes and ears of the full board" in the realm of corporate planning and keep the board informed through minutes of committee meetings, other written reports, and oral presentations at meetings of the full board. They surely monitor corporate performance against plans and monitor the adequacy and quality of the planning system. And they make recommendations to the full board that action be taken—namely, the approval of objectives, strategies and plans. But planning committees are not, as a rule, expected to act for the full board.

Keeping the full board informed is a responsibility emphasized by several planning committee members. Traditionally, they say, most boards have not made an effective contribution to corporate planning, because they have not understood either the basic purposes and concepts of planning or, perhaps more important, the nature of the component businesses of the companies of which they are directors. The planning committee can and does serve to educate other outside board members about these topics, thus enabling those directors to fulfill their responsibilities more adequately. This end is accomplished not only by minutes and reports submitted by the committee to the full board and ensuing discussions at board meetings, but also by a custom, adopted by some committees, of inviting nonmembers to attend committee meetings. One committee routinely schedules the attendance of one nonmember outside director at its monthly meetings. Each of the nonmembers participates on a rotating basis.

Practices of planning committees in passing along to the full board reports and plans prepared for the committee by management are not uniform. At one firm, the corporate planning director submits an annual report to the committee. Before this document goes to the full board, it is subject to alteration by the committee. Similarly, at another firm it is only after the committee has had an opportunity to modify business and financing plans placed before it by management that these plans are presented to the full board—and in revised form if the committee has chosen to exercise this prerogative. At a third company, on the other hand, management plans and proposals that are submitted to the committee are later transmitted unchanged to the full board, together with comments of committee members.

Changed Emphasis

Some planning committees have undergone changes in emphasis, according to those describing them. (Several other committees are so new that it can be inferred that insufficient time has passed for change to have occurred.) Here are verbatim descriptions of such changes as have occurred:

"More attention to strategic planning."
(A diversified company)

* * *

"Spending more time on future planning and longer range policy—less on day-to-day concerns."
(A bank)

* * *

"Now management and the board committee concentrate more on strategies for various markets instead of on individual products or product lines."
(A utility)

* * *

"Many of the sessions are joint meetings with the Finance Committee to discuss long-range strategy and business plans, since both committees are involved. As outside members become increasingly familiar with core businesses, considerably more time is spent on long-range planning for new activities and various long-term strategic options open to the company. Due to the chairman's influence, meetings are becoming less structured,

---

[2]Jeremy Bacon and James K. Brown, *Corporate Directorship Practices: Role, Selection and Legal Status of the Board.* The Conference Board, Report 646, 1975, pp. 99-100.

with more opportunity for discussion by outside directors as opposed to formal presentations by inside directors."

(A manufacturer)

* * *

"Once management, the committee, and, subsequently, the full board had agreed on first principles, so to speak—the mission, basic objectives, and strategy of the company; acquisitions philosophy; needed organizational changes; and the balance between national and international business—for several years the committee focused on the businesses to be sold, and new ones to be acquired, in order to achieve the desired direction for the firm. These transactions having been consummated, the committee is now concentrating on issues pertaining to internal growth."

(A manufacturer)

Chapter 3
Membership and Meetings

HERE are some vital statistics gathered in this inquiry about 29 board planning committees.

- All but two of the committees were formed after 1971. The two exceptions (both companies are utilities) were constituted in the 1960's.
- On most of these committees, outside or non-management directors form a majority. Four of the committees are composed entirely of outside directors. And in three others there is equal representation of outsiders and insiders. Insiders predominate on only one committee. This pattern of outside-director majorities corresponds to that for longer established, more common, board committees like audit, nominating and compensation.
- Two committees consist of the whole board, insiders and outsiders. The reason for this arrangement at one board, that of a utility, is to provide an opportunity for all directors to get "in-depth updates" on planning issues and to discuss them, which is impossible in regular board meetings, given the other business that must be attended to at those meetings.
- Whether or not the chief executive is a committee member—and he may well not be, even if the committee includes representation from the inside directors—he attends at least some of the meetings of most committees. When the CEO does sit on a committee, it is rare for him to be chairman.
- Most of the companies with board planning committees have a corporate planning staff. But in no instance is the head of that staff a member of the board planning committee (indeed, just one corporate planner in the surveyed companies sits on his company's board). Of course, as a rule that individual attends some or all meetings of the committee, and for a few such committees he or she acts as secretary or performs other staff work.
- The stated frequency of meetings each year ranges from one to twenty-five. But some committees have no fixed schedule, meeting at the call of the chairman or "as required." Some met more frequently in the first year or two of their existence than they have more recently. Others have had the opposite experience, being convened more frequently now than they used to be. Of course, bare-bone figures about meeting frequency do not indicate how much time is spent in meetings (not inconsiderable for some committees), conversations among committee members between meetings, and how much preparation is required.

The table presents details for individual committees.

Who Should Serve

Four planning committee members offer perspectives on qualifications for serving on such a committee. These perspectives, as will be seen, are not entirely consonant.

- In constituting a planning committee, it is desirable to assemble a broad variety of backgrounds and talent to ensure that questions management has not thought of are raised or, at least, that management receives fresh perspectives.
- At least in its early stages, a planning committee should be composed of directors who can spend a great deal of time on committee business. It would not be practical to have the chief executive of another company serve on such a committee, since he would have too many commitments to give committee work its due.

The committee of which the director who expressed these opinions is chairman neatly illustrates them. Since its inception in 1976, it has been made up of four "semi-retired" people: the chairman, a former CEO who is now associated with a major business school and serves several firms as an outside director; a retired executive of the company in question; a retired executive of another firm widely regarded as having one of the best planning systems in U.S. industry; and a professor (the chairman

Table: Details about Planning Committees

Company	Committee Name	Year Formed	Outside Directors	Inside Directors	Total	Number of Meetings Per Year
Manufacturing Companies						
1	Corporate Development	1972	1	3	4	25
2	Corporate Objectives	1973	5	2	7	2
3	Corporate Development	1973	2	2	4	5-6
4	Corporate Planning and Nominating	1976	2	1	3	1-2 as required
5	Business Planning and Strategy	1976	4	0	4	2
6	Long-Range Planning	1977	5	2	7	2-6
7	Strategic Planning	1977	4	4	8	5
8	Management Development and Corporate Planning	1978	4	1	5	6
9	Strategy	1978	2	2	4	2 as a rule
10	Planning	1978	2	2	4	Just 1 to date
11	Corporate Planning and Development	1978	4	1	5	When necessary: about 6 in all so far
12	Investment Review	1978	5	1	6	4 scheduled and several special
13	Strategic Affairs	1979	4	3	7	1
14	Strategic Planning	1979	7	2	9	1
15	Corporate Development	1979	6	1	7	No fixed schedule: 1-3
16	Planning	1980	2	1	3	12
Utilities						
17	Corporate Development	1961	5	1	6	Usually 2
18	Business Review and Planning	1967	7	1	8	2-3
19	Planning	1977	3	2	5	5
20	Corporate Planning and Performance	1978	8	3	11[a]	4
Banks and Bank Holding Companies						
21	Long-Range Planning	1975	5	4	9	On call
22	Policy and Planning	1976	6[b]	1	7	12
23	Planning	1978	3	0	3	2
Other[1]						
24	Long-Range Planning	1974	11	1	12[a]	4-5
25	Policy and Planning	1975	5	1	6	2-4 as required
26	Corporate Planning	1977	6	1	7	About 2
27	Corporate Development	1977	3	2	5	As required
28	Finance and Planning[2]	1978	5	0	5	5-6: when needed
29	Corporate Planning	1980	5	0	5	First meeting yet to be called

[a]This committee includes all directors.

[b]In addition, each of the nonmember outside directors attends committee meetings on a rotating basis; see page 8.

[1]In order, these companies are engaged in mining, manufacturing, and shipping; business services; manufacturing, rail transport, and real estate; life insurance; air transport; and financial services.

[2]Before 1978 there were separate finance and planning committees.

acknowledges that the professor would not like to think of himself as semi-retired).

• To be an effective committee member, an outside director has to be experienced in both planning and management development, a rare breed. This almost always means that the member ought to be a CEO or a former CEO, or possess other unusual qualifications, like experience as a business educator. (On the other hand, a CEO who is a member of two planning committees of other boards says it is a mistake to assume that outside directors who are CEO's of their own firms are experts in strategic planning.)

Rotation of Members

Those who hold opinions like all but the last of those just set forth would, of course, argue against regular rotation of committee members. Among the committees about which information was gathered in interviews, there is no scheduled rotation of members, though turnover has occurred in some. Several committees are patently so new that the question of rotation has not come up.

Chapter 4
Does Your Board Need a Planning Committee?

CHAPTER 1 summarized the pros and cons of board planning committees articulated by a professor and two chief executive officers, and described specific circumstances leading to decisions on whether or not to create them. This chapter offers evaluations of such committees in terms of business, organizational or management settings in which such committees may be appropriate and those settings in which they may not. The evaluations are those of study contributors.

When Planning Committees Are Suitable....

Here is a list of situations in which respondents indicate a board planning committee is appropriate:

• When a new chief executive takes office—especially if (1) that individual is recruited from another organization, or (2) his or her predecessor remains on the board and enjoys strong influence with the other directors.

• When the chief executive needs assurance or the board is uneasy about corporate direction. A planning committee may be particularly useful in a company whose diverse interests make it hard to define its mission and determine a proper course for its future.

• When no formal planning process exists, but there is a recognized need for one. This is likely to obtain in a smaller company, one respondent remarks; when it does, a board planning committee may well function like a consultant.

• When management's self-discipline is insufficient for it to carry out its always difficult, easily postponable, responsibility for planning. A committee is called for in these circumstances because—to repeat a point made earlier—the full board has too many other commitments for it to exercise this disciplinary role.

• When the nature of the company's business is such that management must concentrate on daily tactical decisions, and thus has little time for planning.

• When the company is confronted with revolutionary, not evolutionary, change—for example, in technology or industry economics.

• When a company has completed a major merger with a firm in a different industry. One respondent not affiliated in any way with either firm suggested that with the acquisition of Pullman, a bigger company than itself, Wheelabrator-Frye ought to constitute a board planning committee to help management decide what to do with, as he phrased it, its "monstrous and unwieldy new member."

... And When They Are Not

Most of the circumstances in which a planning committee would not be appropriate, according to study participants, are, not surprisingly, the opposite of those that indicate the advisability of constituting such a committee.

• When planning is well-established and accepted and the board is long accustomed to review plans at regular intervals. One CEO, the second successor to the one who had started formal planning at his company over ten years ago, maintains that this is the situation in his firm and that he and his board "wouldn't know what to do with a planning committee."

• In a company engaged in a business or businesses of narrow scope or essential stability.

• In a small company in which management and the directors see one another frequently.

• When another committee in fact functions as a planning committee. One respondent observes that for one of his boards the finance committee acts as a planning committee.

• When a sound planning system is lacking. This should be developed before the board's role is extended to the point of forming a planning committee. (Recall that this is also a circumstance in which a planning committee is said to be appropriate. The respondent who takes the negative view is chairman of one of the largest life insurance companies. In a firm of that stature, he

A Board Not in Need of a Planning Committee

One publicly traded, 120 million-dollar manufacturing firm has a board of five insiders and four outsiders. According to one of the insiders, the president and chief operating officer, this is a hard-working board, deeply involved in company affairs. Although it meets but four times a year, each of the meetings lasts two days. In addition, on at least one other day each quarter the outside directors consult with managers on subjects either designated by management or of interest to individual directors.

The company has put a premium on planning, and to this end it has created and filled the position of vice president, strategic planning services. And the board has an important role to play in planning. The president describes this role as a stair-step approach. The board first signs off on proposed objectives, then strategies, and then action plans. Also, the board monitors progress, very closely and highly specifically with respect to the three-year operating plan, more generally with respect to the ten-year strategic plan.

The president believes that in this company a board planning committee would be irrelevant, given the strong management commitment to planning, the small size of the board, its industriousness, and relatively large number of inside directors. On another board of which he is an outside member, he and his fellow directors are asked to contribute very little to strategic planning and, therefore, are not nearly so constructive a force in shaping the company's future.

thinks that management's having its own house in order is a sine qua non for asking directors to take on planning committee responsibilities.)

• When the full board is satisfied that it adequately understands the company's constituent businesses.

• When a certain degree of agreement about the company's future has been established: Needed acquisitions and divestitures have been made; a pattern of internal growth has been decided upon; there is accord between management and the board as to the firm's proper course.

• When the mission of management is starkly clear. One CEO, who was recruited from the outside to head a foundering enterprise, saw that he had two major jobs: Get rid of the old board and replace it with more competent directors, and dress up the company for sale.

• When the board is small and the company is closely held. One respondent serves on a board consisting of four family members, including the CEO, and three outsiders. The CEO has been pressing for formal planning, but the older family members on the board have resisted it. Thus the full board is the proper forum for directorial participation in planning; a committee would not be appropriate.

• When the composition of the board makes a committee inadvisable. At a major construction company, there are six outside directors and six inside directors, the latter including the CEO, the vice chairman, and four regional vice presidents. According to one of the outside directors, if effective planning is to be introduced and nurtured in that organization—so far it has not been—directorial involvement will require participation of the full board, since the four inside directors who are regional vice presidents will have to do most of the planning.

A caveat: One planning committee member offers a warning about such bodies. A board committee should never add to the bureaucracy and paper work associated with planning, which, in her experience as a consultant, she has found to be excessive in many large corporations.

Recap

What seems clear from the views just presented is that the circumstances of the company in terms of management, board size, the scope and volatility of its businesses, its experience with planning, and internal politics determine the need or lack of need for a planning committee. Beyond this is the suggestion of several of those interviewed that, in time, a planning committee might properly be eliminated. Indeed, this has been the fate of one such committee after a five-year life. Explains a spokesman:

"The committee was formed initially to establish strategy for the development of our bank holding company. It addressed acquisition, capital and human resource requirements. There have been such few changes in these areas that they are now handled by management and the board of directors at its regular meetings."

More generally, if management and the board are in accord about the future course of the enterprise, if a sound planning system is in place, if the firm is making good progress in accordance with well-conceived plans, a planning committee might well become redundant. In a world of apparently incessant change, these are, of course, rather large "ifs."

Appendix

The Corporate Objectives Committee at Texas Instruments Incorporated

The description that follows has been taken from a presentation made by Bryan F. Smith, general director of Texas Instruments Incorporated, on "Role of the Board in the Strategic Process" at a conference on "Strategy for Growth in the 1980's" sponsored by *Business Week* on March 23-24, 1981.[1]

"A stated objective of the company is that a majority of the board, excluding the Chairman and the President, are to be individuals whose primary experience has been other than at TI. Ordinarily, only those board members who serve as Chairman or President are employees of the company. At present, two of our twelve directors, the President and the Chairman, are TI employees, and six have never been employed by the company.

"All ten of our nonexecutive board members are presently designated as general directors, and as such are required to assume board duties (including membership on committees, chairmanship of committees, and optional additional activities in TI's direct interests) with a minimum time commitment of approximately 30 days per year. Actually annual time commitments for general directors presently range from 30 to 75 days, and corresponding fees, exclusive of expenses, range from $46,500 to $90,375.

"The activities of the TI board include attendance at monthly and special board meetings, attendance at corporate planning meetings, and occasional visits to TI plant and office locations. To assure the desired relationship between the board and the operating organization, TI expects most board members to attend some of the scheduled operating organization meetings, internally known as Quarterly Financial Reviews, at which the activities and performance of the various product groups are summarized by management. . . .

"At TI, the committees of the board are expected to hold from three to seven meetings, of varying duration, each year. Each general director is currently expected to devote approximately 10 to 18 days each year to committee work. Currently, we have six committees of the board: Audit, Board Organization and Nominating, Finance, Compensation, Corporate Objectives, and Stockholder Relations. . . .

Directors' Involvement in Planning

"Involving people and providing incentives for good work are essential for encouraging people to make a contribution at all levels of the company. Harnessing their creativity and developing an environment conducive to innovation requires top management's and the board's active participation in long-range planning while being careful not to stifle initiative. . . .

"The Corporate Objectives Committee of the board participates on a regular basis in the company's strategic planning process. In this capacity, it counsels management on the establishment of long-range goals for TI, assesses plans for meeting such goals, and evaluates outside technological and economic influences on the company's future. . . .

"The board's role in the [planning] process as stated in the charter of the Corporate Objectives Committee (see page 16) is to review and evaluate (a) the revisions in the corporate objective and the business objectives; (b) the allocation of the company's resources to those areas that offer potential for profitable growth relative to the requirements of the corporate objective; (c) matching resources to opportunities. The committee also reviews major trends in technology and their effect on the company's operations; the company's technological

---

[1] For more information on the unusual structure of TI's board and the reasons for it, see Jeremy Bacon and James K. Brown, *Corporate Directorship Practices: Role, Selection and Legal Status of the Board.* The Conference Board, Report 646, 1975, pp. 37-39.

capabilities in comparison with the competition; and management's plan to achieve the business objectives and the corporate objective and its progress against those plans. In total, in the course of a working year the Corporate Objectives Committee members spend approximately 10 days working on these matters. Although the board through its Corporate Objectives Committee does have an active participation in the process, it is an inherent requirement of the system that the objectives be set and the plans for obtaining them be made by those responsible for carrying out the plans and achieving the objectives, not by a separate planning group.

"In the first quarter of each year, board members attend a Strategic Planning Conference to discuss business opportunities for the next ten years.

"During the first four days of that conference, managers present their current assessments of long-range opportunities and goals, and reassess their strategies for the realization of such goals. In an environment that allows for considerable give and take, board members evaluate management's proposed allocation of the company's resources. . . .

"During the final two days of the conference, board members may attend further meetings with 500 managers from TI's worldwide operations. After the conference, these long-range inputs are assessed and compared with corporate objectives and necessary actions are defined.

"The budgets for various projects, both companywide and in each business objective area, are determined by means of zero-base budgeting, the technique for enforcing the prioritization of each funded project. Each manager's strategic projects are rank-ordered through the assigned budget, along with some backlog of programs.

"Each time such budgets are reviewed and approved, a zero-base ranking of current projects is required along with comparisons to the objective's priorities.

"In the third quarter, the total budget for the forthcoming year is defined and funds are allocated to the business objectives. The managers, in turn, define their tactical programs and rank order them. . . ."

Texas Instruments Incorporated Corporate Objectives Committee: Statement of Responsibilities

1. To stimulate and focus attention of the board of directors on long-range objectives.

2. To assess the strategies and tactics implementing the long-range objectives.

3. To counsel management in the establishment, and a continuous updating, of a broad definition of purpose and goals.

4. To monitor the implementation process of management in the pursuit of overall corporate goals.

5. To study the potential impact that both short-term and long-term economic trends could have on company operations.

6. To appraise the company's technological effort and product leadership positions.

7. To review major trends in technology and their anticipated effect on the company's operations.

8. To assure that the company's resources are being allocated to those technological areas that offer the greatest potential growth to the company as well as major benefits to society.

9. To review the management's assessment of leadership position of present businesses and growth plans of these businesses; to agree upon additional growth goals in light of the foregoing.

10. To review management's plans for additional growth by:

    (a) Establishing a procedure for evaluating growth recommendations against approved guidelines.

    (b) Evaluating the background and qualifications of employees charged with implementing "new" growth.

11. To review the program to measure progress against plans.

Exhibit 1: Functions of Corporate Development Committee—a Utility

(1) Considers and makes recommendations to the board of directors regarding profit opportunities related or unrelated to the electric utility industry.
(2) Reviews and makes recommendations to the board regarding corporate acquisitions or consolidations.
(3) Considers and makes recommendations to the board regarding subsidiary, ancillary or joint investments.
(4) Reviews and makes recommendations to the board regarding sale or other disposition of major components of the company's building and properties.
(5) Reviews and reports to the board regarding the corporate planning function of the company.
(6) Reviews and reports to the board regarding other matters relative to the future direction of the company.

Exhibit 2: Planning Committee—a Bank

RESOLVED, that the board of directors of [the Bank], pursuant to Section 2.9 of the bylaws of the bank, hereby establishes the Planning Committee (the "Planning Committee") as a standing committee of the board of directors composed of not less than three members of the board of directors.

FURTHER RESOLVED, that the Planning Committee shall meet at least twice each calendar year and at such other times as may be necessary upon the call of the chairman of the board of directors, the president or the chairman of the Planning Committee, by notice of the time and place of the meeting given to each member of the Planning Committee at least five days before the meeting if such notice is sent by mail or at least 24 hours before the meeting if such notice is given by telegram, telephone or personal delivery to the member's address on the bank's records.

FURTHER RESOLVED, that the duties and responsibilities of the Planning Committee shall be:

(a) to receive and study reports (whether prepared at the request of the Planning Committee or otherwise) on present and future trends in the areas of banking and finance and make such recommendations and plans based on such reports and studies as may be appropriate to insure that the bank and its subsidiaries are prepared to compete effectively in the future;

(b) to request, receive and evaluate studies and reports made by various groups, committees or individuals, whether or not associated with the bank, on matters of significance to the development of short- and long-range plans for the bank and its subsidiaries; and

(c) to recommend to the board of directors for approval short- and long-range plans for the bank and its subsidiaries. . . .

FURTHER RESOLVED, that the presence of at least two members of the Planning Committee shall be necessary for the transaction of business at all meetings of the Planning Committee.

Exhibit 3: Management Development and Corporate Planning Committee—a Manufacturer

COMMITTEE FUNCTIONS

1. Review the current executive organization structure and personnel in relation to the continuing organizational requirements of the company.

2. Advise and consult with the company's Chief Executive Officer regarding the plans and implementation of such plans for orderly succession of directors and to the office of Chairman of the Board and Chief Executive Officer and such other offices as may be directly affected thereby.

3. Advise and consult with the company's Chief Executive Officer regarding (a) improvements in the executive organization structure; (b) future individual management and executive succession development and plans; and (c) such other matters as may be deemed appropriate to provide strong, creative leadership for the company in the future.

4. Assure itself and the board of directors that management has developed, maintains and is implementing tactical and strategic plans which will provide for the future growth and success of the company.

5. Keep itself knowledgeable about the various plans of the company; the goals and methods for achieving such goals contained in such plans; and the actions taken or to be taken in order to implement such plans.

6. Review and critique the progress and successes or failures achieved by such plans, and, if appropriate, suggest to management corrective changes.

7. Constructively challenge the business, economic, social, political, financial or other theses or assumptions which underlie the company's plans in order to assure the success of those plans.

8. Review management's justifications for continuing current company businesses in light of the particular problems, challenges and opportunities associated with the future of those businesses.

9. Conduct such investigations and interviews as it deems necessary and appropriate to fulfill its functions.

10. It is not the purpose of this committee to assume any of management's responsibility for the day-to-day functioning of the company.

Exhibit 4: Delegation of Authority to the Strategic Planning Committee of the Board of Directors—a Manufacturer

— To define and review periodically the broad corporate strategies which will be followed in the pursuit of the broad corporate objectives approved by the board of directors.
— To annually review the strategic planning process of the management of the corporation and report its evaluation and recommendation to the board of directors.
— To provide the management of the corporation with its insights on those facets of the future external environment with which the committee members are familiar.

Exhibit 5: Charge for a Manufacturer's Strategy Committee

The Strategy Committee shall advise management and recommend to the board of directors actions necessary to determine future company activities and organization. This committee shall be constituted annually by the board of directors at its organizational meeting. Membership shall be limited to board members.

Specifically, the committee is charged with determining what the company should be doing (in the future) within the following areas: a) products and services; b) geographical markets; c) customers served; d) organizational capability supporting those products and markets; e) its growth and return; and f) its allocation of resources.

Exhibit 6: Guide for Policy and Planning Committee—a Bank

The first of the joint monthly Policy and Planning Meetings of the Executive Committees of the holding company and the bank was held on August 11, 1976, devoted to matters of policy and long-range planning.

The boards of the corporation and the bank, at meetings held on August 29, 1978, by resolution adopted by a majority of the whole boards, approved the continuation of such joint meetings and designated a Policy and Planning Committee comprised of the members of the Executive Committee plus two additional outside members of the boards. Meetings shall be held on the second Tuesday of each month, and the President shall preside.

Long-range goals for the corporation and the bank and priorities in attaining such objectives shall be developed by the Policy and Planning Committee in conjunction with senior management, with recommendations to the appropriate board as to the fixing of such goals and the methods for their achievement.

The Policy and Planning Committee shall direct its attention toward issues with long-range implications rather than issues relating to current opportunities or problems. It is contemplated that the role of the committee will continue to be the maintenance of long-range plans for the corporation and the bank against which current or contemplated activities may be tested to ensure consistent and prudent decision making by management and the boards.

Exhibit 7: Functions and Duties of the Planning Committee of the Board of Directors—a Manufacturer

GENERAL

The Planning Committee of the board of directors of the corporation shall be comprised of the Corporate Chief Executive Officer, the Corporate Chief Financial Officer and no fewer than one nonemployee director. Its primary function is to monitor the company's long-range financial and operating objectives to assure that they are consistent with (1) the board of directors' intentions, (2) the company's overall capabilities, and (3) the prevailing markets and economies.

SPECIFIC DUTIES

1) The committee shall become acquainted with and stay apprised of the company's objectives and planning process. This is to be accomplished via two full-day meetings each year. One meeting will be held during the latter portion of the fourth quarter, upon completion of the next year's corporate objectives, and the other during midyear.

2) The committee shall keep the board of directors advised of the company's long-range financial and operating objectives.

3) The committee shall become acquainted with and stay apprised of the company's resources to assure that the company's objectives are attuned to their availability.

4) The committee shall become acquainted with and stay apprised of the conditions of the markets and economies in which the company is involved.

5) The committee shall be on the alert and make appropriate recommendations for potential new business opportunities.

Exhibit 8: Functions of a Business Review and Planning Committee—a Utility

To review and make recommendations to the board of directors with respect to performance in business areas and to review and make recommendations in the board with respect to the company's long-range business plans.

Exhibit 9: Functions of a Long-Range Planning Committee—a Bank Holding Company

Long-Range Planning Committee—consists of directors appointed by the board of directors, who are not members of the Long-Term Incentive Committee, to plan the company's activities and operations and to coordinate the activities and operations of its subsidiaries on a long-range basis, including domestic and foreign operations.

Exhibit 10: Bylaw Statement Re: Corporate Planning and Performance Committee—a Utility

A Corporate Planning and Performance Committee is hereby established. Such committee shall consist of all members of the board of directors. The chairman of the committee shall be elected by a majority vote of the committee members from among those members who are not employees or officers of the company at the first committee meeting following the annual meeting of stockholders, except a vacancy in said positions may be filled at any time. Said committee shall meet at least quarterly at such time and place as it determines, and at the call of the chairman or any other member of the committee. Such meeting may be held on a day separate from or the same as the regular monthly meeting of the board of directors.

The responsibility of said committee shall be to examine corporate planning and performance, including the review of such items as sales and load forecasts, operating and construction budgets, financing programs, and rate matters.

Exhibit 11: Board Resolution Concerning a Corporate Development Committee—a Manufacturing Company

RESOLVED, that hereafter the composition, powers and authority of the Corporate Development Committee (the "Committee"), established on October 30, 1979, shall:

(a) be composed of at least three directors who shall have a chairman designated by the board of directors;

(b) meet at the discretion of the committee with appropriate officers and employees of the corporation to review the corporation's programs relating to:

  (1) development of present lines of business,
  (2) establishment of new lines of business not now contained in the corporate portfolio,
  (3) elimination of existing lines of business;

(c) function as a committee of the board of directors in reviewing acquisitions and divestitures of corporate assets which require board approval;

(d) function as a committee of the board of directors in receiving and reviewing proposals for mergers or business consolidations;

(e) report to the board of directors concerning activities and recommendations of the committee;

(f) be available to undertake other projects, tasks and responsibilities as may be assigned from time to time by the board of directors.

Exhibit 12: A Board Resolution about a Corporate Planning Committee—a Manufacturer

FURTHER RESOLVED that the powers and duties of the Corporate Planning Committee of the Board of Directors shall be:

(1) to review and consider management's program for the development and succession of management, identifying and developing those rare individuals who have character, intelligence, motivation, education, stamina, and personality to be top caliber executives,

(2) to review and recommend to the board all mergers and acquisitions that fall within the corporation's defined fields of interest,

(3) to periodically review with management the corporation's strategic planning.

Exhibit 13: Function and Chairman's Responsibilities: a Policy and Planning Committee—a Business Service Firm

FUNCTION AND CHAIRMAN'S RESPONSIBILITIES: *Resolutions adopted at Board of Directors' Meeting....*

RESOLVED, that the operating procedures of the Policy and Planning Committee shall have responsibility for reviewing major business policies and strategic plans for the company, developing recommendations and rendering reports with respect thereto to the board, and specifically:

1) The responsibility of the Chairman of the Policy and Planning Committee will be that of being advisory and consultative to the board of directors and the Chief Executive Officer;

2) The Chief Executive Officer has the responsibility for implementing plans and programs adopted by the board of directors;

3) It is recognized that the Chairman of the Policy and Planning Committee must keep informed and be kept informed of developments of significance in the company and that he will have direct communications with appropriate staff, but that such communications will not interfere with or hinder the Chief Executive Officer in fulfilling his responsibilities;

and further

RESOLVED, that the Policy and Planning Committee shall:

1) Regularly review management's long-term strategic plans, including capital requirements, manpower requirements and general business strategies for the company, and make recommendations thereon to the board;

2) Review and recommend to the board, based on presentations of management, recommendations, annual goals and objectives for the growth and development of each of the major divisions and for the company as a whole, consistent with the strategic plan. Plans submitted by management should include recommendations regarding capital requirements, manpower requirements, and general business strategies;

3) Review and report its conclusions to the board on how annual plans have been translated into operating results;

4) Be responsible for reviewing and recommending to the board all acquisitions and divestitures of assets proposed by management in excess of $1 million and highlighting for the board where such acquisitions and divestitures fit within the framework of the long-term plan. Where the recommendations represent deviations from the plan, the committee should indicate the reasons for such deviation in making its recommendations to the board;

5) Review major business policies and, as appropriate, make recommendations to the board;

6) Be prepared to become involved in specific major and critical business situations where the company might benefit from the experience and perspective of the members.

MEETING DATE: Held as required